HELLO KITTY®

SWEET, HAPPY, FUN BOOK!

HELLO KITTY®

SWEET, HAPPY, FUN BOOK!

A SNEAK PEEK INTO HER SUPERCUTE WORLD

Sanrio®

RUNNING PRESS
PHILADELPHIA · LONDON

Written by Marie Moss

First published in the United States in
2010 by Running Press Book Publishers.

Printed in China

9 8 7 6 5 4 3 2 1
Digit on the right indicates the number of this printing

Library of Congress Control Number: 2010923296

ISBN 978-0-7624-3770-2

Hello Kitty Sweet, Happy, Fun Book! is produced by becker&mayer!,
Bellevue, Washington.
www.beckermayer.com

Editorial: Amy Wideman
Image Research: Jessica Eskelsen
Design: Kasey Free
Production Coordination: Diane Ross and Leah Finger
License Acquisition: Josh Anderson
Art Direction: Yumi Nakamura and Andrew Yang

Running Press Book Publishers
2300 Chestnut Street
Philadelphia, PA 19103-4371

Visit us on the Web!
www.runningpress.com

CONTENTS

INTRODUCTION

Despite modest beginnings over thirty years ago in Japan as a simple character sketch adorning stationery and small gifts, Hello Kitty's charm and universal appeal quickly elevated her to one of the world's most recognizable figures.

Internationally known and loved, Hello Kitty has cheerfully interpreted lifestyle trends for her friends and admirers, in the form of supercute clothing items, accessories, and home furnishings, for several years. She is also a steadfast symbol of fun, friendship, and happiness. From her very own amusement park and retail stores to Hello Kitty airplanes and karaoke clubs, Hello Kitty gives fans a reason to smile.

HELLO, HELLO KITTY!

Hello Kitty was first created by Sanrio in Japan in 1974. Setting out to create a character that would appeal to both children and adults, Sanrio first envisioned a seated Hello Kitty in profile with head turned full-on. Her simple outfit was comprised of blue overalls with white buttons and a bright red bow worn atop her left ear.

Hello Kitty is the height of five apples, and the weight of three. Her blood type is A.

From the start, Hello Kitty was drawn with simple wide-set eyes, six whiskers, a tail, and no mouth.

Some of her hobbies include baking, traveling, learning new things, playing sports, and spending time with her friends.

KITTY'S PROFILE

いつもそばにいるからこそ、知っていてほしいキティのすべてを大公開！
知ればきっと、あなたの中のキティワールドが広がって、ますます仲良くなれるはず。

名 前

キティ・ホワイト。「ハロー キティ」はフルネームではなく、愛称です。名前の由来は、『鏡の国のアリス』に出てくるこねこちゃんからつけられました。

体 重

りんご3個分。

得意な科目

国語（キティは、ロンドンっ子だから英語が国語ですね）、美術、音楽。

好きな言葉

「友情」

宝 物

持っているとラッキーなことが起こるカギ。キティとりすのローリーが、森で見つけた秘密の宝物です。

住んでいる所

出身地も住んでいるところも、イギリスのロンドン中心地から20キロほど離れた郊外の小さな街です。車で25分くらいで行くことができます。

誕生日

11月1日生まれ、さそり座。もちろん、双子のミミィと一緒です。

血液型

A型。

身 長

りんごをタテに5個並べた高さ。

71 FACE WIDTH

56 FULL LENGTH OF HEAD

40.5

34.6 DISTANCE BETWEEN EYES

4.5 LENGTH OF NOSE

11

100 KITTY'S HEIGHT

33 LENGTH OF TORSO

11 LENGTH OF FEET

41 WIDTH OF TORSO

好きな食べ物

ママの作ったアップルパイ。

一番最初のお友達は？

それは金魚さん。キティのデビューグッズ、プチパースにも一緒に登場しています。

コレクション

ちっちゃくてかわいい物。リボンやヘアアクセサリー。

将来の夢

ピアニストか詩人になること。

特 技

クッキー作り。ホワイト家直伝のレシピをママに教えてもらっているから、とびきりおいしいのです。

毎朝することは？

それはおひげのお手入れ。毎朝7時半に起きて歯を磨いた後、これを欠かさないのが、ねこの女のコの大事なみだしなみなのです。

...wears a bow on ... their parents can

HELLO, FRIENDS AND FAMILY

Hello Kitty, a symbol of friendship, is very close to her friends and family. At the base of Hello Kitty's family tree are parents George and Mary White (introduced to the world in 1976) and Anthony (Grandpa) and Margaret (Grandma) White (who made their debut in 1979). Hello Kitty, Mimmy, and the rest of the family live in a house in the suburbs of London, England. Papa is known for his sense of humor but also enjoys reading the daily newspaper. Mama designs and makes all of Hello Kitty and Mimmy's clothing and is known for her yummy fruit pies. (Hello Kitty's favorite is apple.) Patriarch Grandpa, an alumnus of prestigious schools, also happens to be a talented painter. Grandma, for her part, enjoys doing embroidery.

GEORGE WHITE

ANTHONY WHITE

MARY WHITE

MIMMY WHITE

KITTY WHITE

MARGARET WHITE

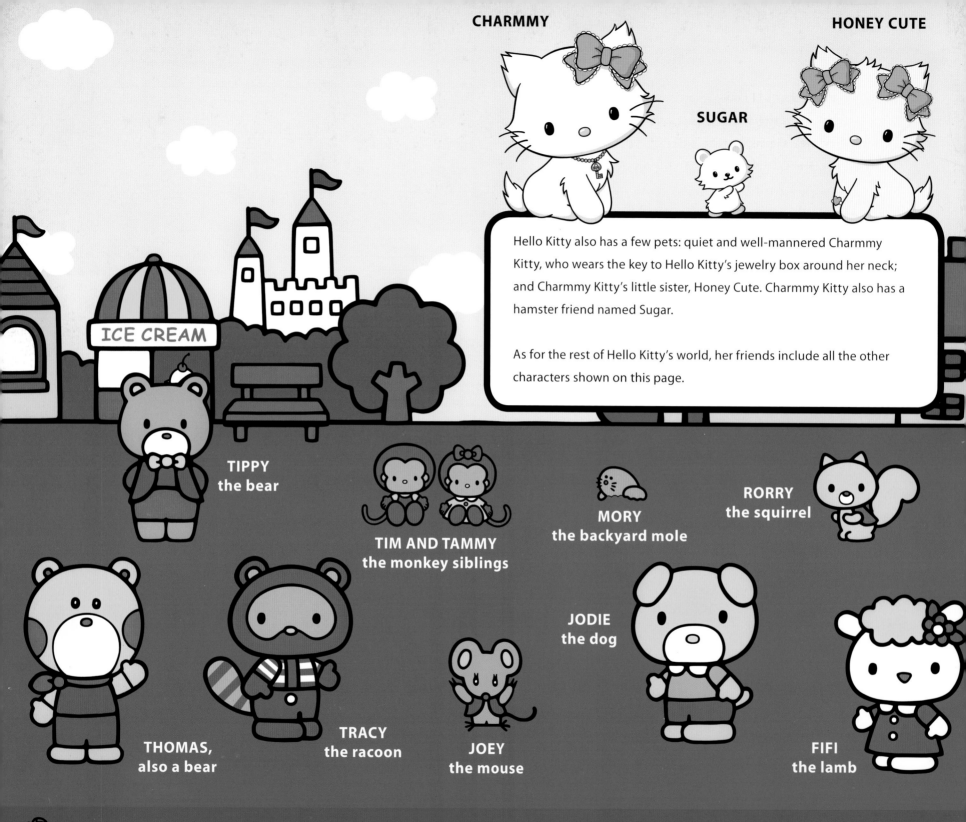

CHARMMY

SUGAR

HONEY CUTE

Hello Kitty also has a few pets: quiet and well-mannered Charmmy Kitty, who wears the key to Hello Kitty's jewelry box around her neck; and Charmmy Kitty's little sister, Honey Cute. Charmmy Kitty also has a hamster friend named Sugar.

As for the rest of Hello Kitty's world, her friends include all the other characters shown on this page.

ICE CREAM

TIPPY
the bear

TIM AND TAMMY
the monkey siblings

MORY
the backyard mole

RORRY
the squirrel

THOMAS,
also a bear

TRACY
the racoon

JOEY
the mouse

JODIE
the dog

FIFI
the lamb

Dear Daniel is Hello Kitty's boyfriend. Named for a character in the 1971 English film *Melody*, Daniel resembles Hello Kitty, with wide-set eyes and no visible mouth. He wears jeans, T-shirts, and suspenders, and has spiky hair. Dear Daniel is adventurous and frequently goes on safari in Africa with his photographer dad. Hello Kitty writes him letters using her favorite letter sets and pens.

Others in Hello Kitty's world include Mr. Policeman, the Bus Driver, the local medical doctor, a candy shop proprietor in a striped dress and paper crown, and a downtown diner chef who serves yummy grilled hamburgers and hot dogs.

DEAR DANIEL

MR. POLICEMAN

BUS DRIVER

Hello Kitty's friends and family appear on a wide array of collectible items, along with Hello Kitty. Her family, Dear Daniel, Tippy the Bear, and all the rest can be found on everything from lunch boxes to keychains to colorful wooden houses and figures.

HELLO, COLLECTIBLES

With the "small gift, big smile" concept at heart, Sanrio's many offerings of Hello Kitty collectibles guarantee fans an eternal quest for what's next. Tomorrow's Hello Kitty incarnation is today's topic of speculation. With hundreds of new Hello Kitty items offered every month, and just as many rotating off the shelves, super fans are kept on their toes.

And while "small gift, big smile" might suggest that a significant portion of Hello Kitty collectibles are small (i.e., cell phone charms, stickers, push pins, mechanical pens), the ever-expanding catalog includes plenty of larger items, too (microwave ovens, snowboards, pet carriers, golf clubs, and more). There's something for every Hello Kitty collector at every budget, even if that budget allows for diamond jewelry.

There are so many Hello Kitty collectibles that it is possible to spend an entire day moving from one Hello Kitty product to another. Imagine . . .

. . . *You wake up in Hello Kitty pajamas, toasty and warm beneath your Hello Kitty sheets and blankets. You turn to your Hello Kitty bedside table to turn off your Hello Kitty alarm clock. You rise and shine as you step into your Hello Kitty slippers, and head for the shower where your bathroom is stocked with Hello Kitty toiletries, shower curtain, toothpaste, and toothbrush. Out of the shower, it's time to dry off with your Hello Kitty bath towel, to comb your hair with your Hello Kitty brush, and to apply Hello Kitty lotion and cosmetics.*

Warm toast with Hello Kitty's face pops up from your Hello Kitty toaster, while you sip juice from a Hello Kitty juice cup poured from a matching pitcher. Dressed in Hello Kitty T-shirt, jeans, and sneakers, accessorized with Hello Kitty earrings, pendant necklace, purse, and bookbag, you head for the garage where your Hello Kitty Daihatsu hatchback car—next to your Hello Kitty retro bicycle, complete with Hello Kitty bell and basket—is parked (and decked out in Hello Kitty car-seat covers and air freshener). You head to school or the office, where your desktop supplies include Hello Kitty pens, notepads, staplers, and even a Hello Kitty laptop.

Later that day, you answer your Hello Kitty cell phone to accept a picnic lunch date, where you'll serve snacks from Hello Kitty plastic containers stored neatly inside a Hello Kitty picnic hamper complete with Hello Kitty silverware, napkins, cookies, and even Hello Kitty-shaped pasta salad.

That afternoon, you plan a birthday party for a friend based entirely on Hello Kitty, including plates, cups, napkins, balloons, a piñata, and goodie bags filled with Hello Kitty treats. And you daydream about the wedding you will someday have, with Hello Kitty champagne flutes, place cards, wedding gift bags, and a Hello Kitty wedding gown.

Maria's biggest Hello Kitty obsession is collecting as many of the hundreds of Asunarosya's Gotochi Hello Kitty charms as she can find. These tiny, trinket-like figurines depict Hello Kitty in many incarnations, including Hello Kitty as corn on the cob, a slushy ice drink, a potted cactus, and a peapod. The Gotochi Kitty collection was first launched in 1998 with the introduction of "Lavender Kitty," a Hello Kitty designed to represent Hokkaido, the northern region of Japan. Demand for the Lavender Hello Kitty collection grew, and it would soon include many other souvenirs like mascots, stationery, and cell phone charms.

To celebrate the launch of the expanded Lavender Hello Kitty collection, the entire souvenir shop in the New Chitose Airport in Sapporo (Hokkaido) was dyed in pure lavender!

Building upon this success, Asunarosya continued their collaboration with Sanrio and began offering a Gotochi Hello Kitty for regions in Japan. Every year, Asunarosya introduces more than three hundred new collectibles. They have even offered a Gotochi Hello Kitty representing U.S. travel destinations like Florida and New York City.

The task of finding and collecting them all can become a full-time job, as the purchase of one cute Hello Kitty-as-sushi piece can be the catalyst for an all-out, *gotta-have-'em!* feeling. In fact, this scenario is played out for many Hello Kitty fans amassing all kinds of Hello Kitty collectibles. From figurines to giant Hello Kitty plush, a mission to acquire all that is available from one collection or of one type of item in particular is often sparked with the very first Hello Kitty gift or purchase.

Maria, like many fans, manages the sheer quantity of her collection by making an effort to purchase items she can actually use, not just put on a shelf. She collects bedding, blankets, washcloths, aprons, mugs, and clothing—all pieces with a purpose. Her largest Hello Kitty piece is her structured rolling luggage—"Though I dream of owning the bicycle, television, and Fender guitar!" she adds.

While she would love to someday organize a fan trip back to Japan to visit Sanrio's Puroland (the giant indoor theme park located in Tama New Town, Tokyo), she stays content by keeping up her blog. "It is a place for me to acknowledge my serious Hello Kitty addiction and to meet other fans all around the world," Maria says. Through the blog, this self-proclaimed "Hello Kitty Junkie" shares photos of her Hello Kitty finds as well as notes on news of Hello Kitty's global adventures. Friends and fans, many of whom declare Maria as Hello Kitty's *ichiban* (or "number one") fan, reply with photos and information about their own collections.

Among this worldwide community, Maria's kindred spirit can be found in Canadian Emily H., who discovered Hello Kitty as a child when her father would return from business trips to Japan with tiny Hello Kitty treasures. "My favorite souvenir was a Hello Kitty digital watch, which I kept inside my 'Sanrio drawer' filled with everything I had collected."

Emily's special drawer was over three feet long, with enough space for all of her favorite finds. Emily eventually segued into a more serious devotion to Hello Kitty, celebrating her own Japanese heritage with every new addition. "My background and my passion for Japanese dance inspires much of what I collect today, and I am particularly interested in items wherein Hello Kitty is dressed in a traditional Japanese kimono," she shares. "I like collecting pieces that show Hello Kitty doing a well-known Japanese dance, Fujimusume. I also like images of Hello Kitty in black hair worn in traditional Japanese style."

Like Maria, Emily reaches out to other fans through her blog, and dreams of her own trip to Sanrio's Puroland or Sanrio's outdoor theme park, Harmonyland.

Back in the states, Hello Kitty fan Allison W. of New York City shares how she kept all of her Hello Kitty collectibles safely tucked inside a special box in her sock drawer. Today, twenty-five years later, she still devotes apartment space to her treasures. "I recall being instantly smitten with Hello Kitty upon having discovered her for the first time at the local mall. This girl was no Barbie, no My Little Pony! Even my grandmother, who was often my date for the day, could appreciate the almost painful cuteness of Hello Kitty," Allison shares. "I even loved the sweet plastic smell of the Sanrio shop, filled to the ceiling with collectibles. To this day, I can still recall that wonderful plastic smell that conjures up memories of my weekly trips to the mall with my grandmother to see what was new and fabulous with our friend, Hello Kitty."

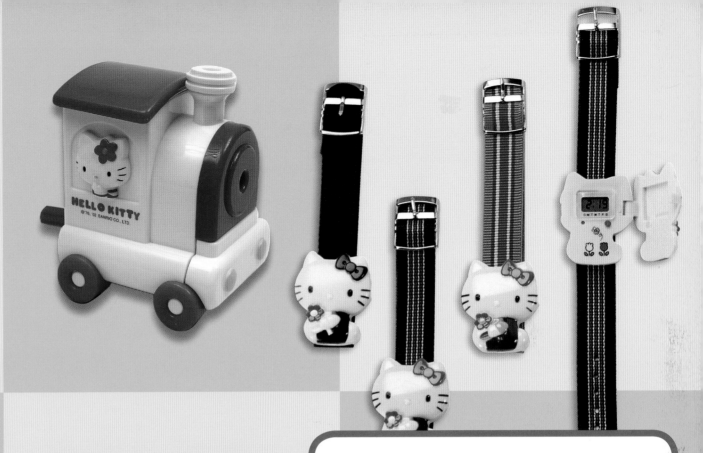

And some fans collect Hello Kitty in an even more permanent way: Jacques L. of California was so smitten with his Hello Kitty-loving girlfriend, Ellen O., that he not only proposed to her by presenting a Kimora Lee Simmons for Hello Kitty diamond ring—he also went the extra mile by having a local tattoo artist design a Hello Kitty tattoo for him to match Ellen's.

Jacques, Ellen, and their fellow fans are voicing what Sanrio and company founder Shintaro Tsuji have made their mission: for Hello Kitty to symbolize friendship and happiness, and to bring a smile to kids and adults all around the world.

DESIGN EVOLUTION: A TIMELINE

1975

Hello, Hello Kitty

The very first Hello Kitty item—a clear, snap-shut coin purse—debuts, featuring the classic seated pose. Slippers, pencils, dishes, and a pencil case are soon added, and so begins a collecting craze like no other. This unprecedented phenom, not based on an existing television, film, or book character, is about to take the world by storm.

1976

Standing Tall

An upright Hello Kitty appears on collectibles including stationery and accessories. Hello Kitty arrives in the United States!

1977

Safe Travels

Hello Kitty appears on a bicycle, in a school bus, flying a plane, and as a train conductor. Desk supplies and travel-sized grooming items like brushes, combs, travel bags, and toothbrushes continue to grow in numbers, gaining popularity with both children and adults.

1978

Summertime

Hello Kitty celebrates the sun in a playful anchor romper and flip-flops. She's shown standing up, running, and even riding a dolphin.

1979

Outdoor Fun

Hello Kitty adorns pom-pom ski caps, scarves, and terry cloth wristbands.

1980

I ♥ the '80s

Sanrio welcomes the new decade with a flip-up, die-cut, digital Hello Kitty watch; over one million are sold. Hello Kitty playing tennis is called out on other products.

1981

Around the Kitchen

Hello Kitty appears on items like a panini sandwich maker, rice bowls and chopsticks, and various electronics. The first Hello Kitty movie, *Kitty and Mimmy's New Umbrella*, is released in Japan.

1982

Sweet Treats

Hello Kitty's love of candy extends to a collectible, refillable gumball machine.

1983

Picnic Perfect

The Pleasantime red-and-white checked gingham collection is perfect for picnics. Hello Kitty collectible pins also join the scene, and Hello Kitty is named Child Ambassador of UNICEF.

1984

Take a Photo

Fans find Hello Kitty's flight bags and luggage tags irresistible. New, too, are Hello Kitty collectibles using photo reel imagery.

1985

New Hues

Various brown shades are introduced on many items.

1986

Classic Bold

Hello Kitty's face dominates much of the latest collection, going back to a bolder, more classic look.

1987

Draw With Me

A white outlined version of Hello Kitty is introduced. It appears on a variety of collectibles against a black background.

1988

In Full Plaid

The trend is tartan, with offerings that include wallets, tote bags, and room décor. American television debuts *Hello Kitty Fairy Tale Theater* on CBS-TV.

1989

Color Whirl!

Primary colors add a "pop art" look to the Hello Kitty collection. Fan favorites include comic-like artwork on stationery supplies.

1990

Fashion Statement

Hello Kitty appears on gummy slip-on shoes, striped suspenders, and shiny wallets. A background of a snowy day decorates many collectibles, as does a Hello Kitty dressed like Santa Claus. Puroland opens!

1991

In Full Bloom

A flower power design takes shape, and Hello Kitty's polka dot collection is introduced. Harmonyland opens!

1992

Punched-up Pastels

Rosy pinks, lemon yellows, and trendy teals turn up in flower-, fruit-, and heart-shaped design collectibles. Favorites include zip-up pencil cases, pen pal sets, and vanity-top pieces.

1993

Baby Time

Hello Kitty and boyfriend Dear Daniel turn up as babies dressed in pastels. And for the first time ever, Hello Kitty sports a flower hair accessory instead of her traditional hair bow.

1994

Fruit Mix

Going tropical, Hello Kitty surrounds herself in pineapples, bananas, and cherries. She also appears dressed as a nurse in cap and uniform.

1995

Back to Basics

A favorite with fans, Hello Kitty's flower power design from 1991 makes a comeback. She also models favorite color pink.

1996

Prized Possessions

Fans rush to stores for Hello Kitty's cool new 35mm camera.

1997

Tasty Delights

Strawberry-themed collectibles are introduced, as is Hello Kitty Angel. Mermaid Hello Kitty appears, and collectors begin to find Hello Kitty dressed in traditional Japanese attire.

1998

Fresh Picks

Pastel balloon-like flowers beckon fans to think pink.

1999

Above the Clouds

Hello Kitty Angel takes to the skies on a unicorn.

2000

Shining Star

Hello Kitty Fairy makes her debut, complete with sparkly star tiara, sash, shiny gown, and magic wand. Also, fast food giant McDonald's offers its first Hello Kitty Happy Meal.

2001

Let's Get Together

Sanrio and designer Paul Frank pair up to combine Hello Kitty and Julius the Monkey on accessories. Photo-driven book *Hello Kitty Hello Everything* celebrates 25 years of collectibles.

2002

Famous Friends

Hello Kitty's superstar status is cemented as celebrity friends such as Mariah Carey, Christina Aguilera, Heidi Klum, and Mandy Moore show their love of Hello Kitty to the world.

2003

Designer Fashion

The Hello Kitty Couture Collection by Heatherette appears on the runway.

2004

Papa Brings Home a Pet!

Charmmy Kitty the cat is introduced, along with her younger sister, Honey Cute, and their hamster friend, Sugar. Hello Kitty's image takes a turn on MasterCard debit cards, and Hello Kitty is named UNICEF's Global Special Friend of Children.

2005

Diamonds are Forever

Model and designer Kimora Lee Simmons teams up with Sanrio to launch the diamond Hello Kitty Collection by Kimora Lee Simmons.

2006

To the Letter

Rainbow-colored "bubble" letters spell out Hello Kitty on key chain cases and accessories.

2007

Music & Celebration

Sanrio partners with Cherry Lane to publish music based on Hello Kitty. For the first time, Hello Kitty appears in the iconic Macy's Thanksgiving Day Parade.

2008

Fashionable Pairing

Sanrio teams up with Italian designer Simone Legno for the tokidoki for Hello Kitty collection (*tokidoki* translates from Japanese as "sometimes").

2009

Happy Anniversary!

Sanrio marks Hello Kitty's 35th Anniversary with commemorative merchandise and a global celebration. A chic collaboration with M·A·C Cosmetics, the introduction of iPhone apps, and the multi-dimensional "Three Apples" Exhibit round out the year.

SWEET ON HELLO KITTY

Hello Kitty gum and candy treats have long appealed to sweet-toothed fans. And while the ultimate in satisfying a sweet Hello Kitty craving would be enjoying a sugary menu item from the Hello Kitty Sweets Café in Taipei, Taiwan, you don't have to go that far to fill your pockets with sweets almost too cute to eat.

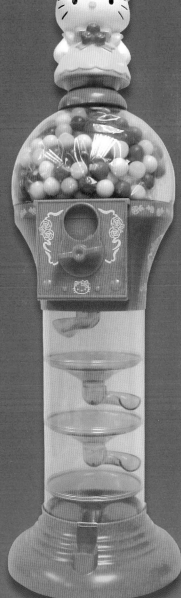

From beaded Hello Kitty candy charm necklaces and bracelets sold at Sanrio boutiques around the country, to Hello Kitty–shaped sugar cookies and chocolate cutouts from New York City's Chinatown neighborhood, Hello Kitty sweets offer much to savor. And that's *after* you've torn past the sweet packaging and graphics that hold them. Fans are especially smitten with Hello Kitty confections sold in collectible packaging; Sanrio's Hello Kitty Full Body PEZ candy dispenser, to name just one example, debuted in the summer of 2009.

HOUSE OF HELLO KITTY

From kitchen appliances to living room décor, if there's something your bedroom, dorm room, apartment, or even your entire *house* requires, Hello Kitty's got it covered.

Like many fans, Renee F. of Connecticut keeps her kitchen stocked with Hello Kitty. Snacks are kept in Hello Kitty plastic storage containers, coffee is brewed in a Hello Kitty coffeemaker, toast crisps in a Hello Kitty toaster, and popcorn kernels burst open in a Hello Kitty popcorn maker. Renee makes space for Hello Kitty wherever she can. Even her grocery list and family photos (including a shot of her meeting—and hugging!—Hello Kitty in a New York Sanrio boutique) command a spot on the refrigerator with Hello Kitty magnets.

And while Hello Kitty devotee Sheena P. of Colorado will never unwrap her precious collection of Hello Kitty toiletries, she keeps them out and prominently displayed. "I called the Grand Hi Lai Hotel in Taiwan to see if I could order any of their Hello Kitty hotel room amenities," she explains. "I managed to get a few things, but I had to work for it, that's for sure! I had to send an authorization form for a credit card and did not have the computer program for it, so I had to download a trial program. It took three hours just to print it out and fax it back—by then it was 4 a.m.! All in the name of my Hello Kitty obsession, but I got the unattainable!" Sheena laughs about the lengthy quest but points out that there is always more to collect.

Fellow fan Anna H. of Washington state sent a pal in Kyoto, Japan on a hunt for Hello Kitty toilet paper, and her New York City–bound brother and his wife on a search for a hoodie displaying Hello Kitty as the Statue of Liberty. "I will collect just about everything Hello Kitty," Anna admits, recalling that the first piece in her collection was a simple coin purse.

As for collector Edward H. of Texas, his interest began with a small Hello Kitty figurine given to him by a friend. While Edward's collection now includes a variety of categories, he is particularly intrigued with home décor pieces with a purpose. From a wall clock to a desk caddy to a bedside lamp to a soap dispenser, Hello Kitty finds a home all around Edward's house.

And a California mystery man known to Hello Kitty bloggers as "HK Guy" is crazy for Hello Kitty mahjong sets. In addition to these, HK Guy's favorite collectibles include a Hello Kitty silver Euro coin set and a highly collectible Hello Kitty Dreamcast video game console by Sega.

The irresistible Hello Kitty plush incarnations fill the shelves, beds, armoires, and mantles of many fans. The coziest of all Hello Kitty collectibles, Hello Kitty plush is available in sizes from as small as a keychain trinket to those that can barely fit through a car door. And since these plush can't be stored away as easily as stationery or silverware, fans prefer to set these huggable collectibles out for admiring, making them Hello Kitty's most popular "home décor" offering.

This is especially true for any limited edition Hello Kitty plush, from the tokidoki "Sandy" cactus girl to the various plush "dressed" as animals to the Hello Kitty items co-branded with Quolomo, Edwin, and other popular labels.

Just ask Lori S. of California, whose home office appears to have been taken over by Hello Kitty plush. "I have over one hundred," Lori says. "Most range in size from about six inches to a foot tall, but I also have a Hello Kitty Momoberry display doll [Hello Kitty's "fancy" collection] that is close to four feet tall and weighs ten pounds. A friend brought it back from Japan for me."

Then there's Marie Angeline Y. of Los Angeles, who also enjoys a large (and globe-crossing) collection. While she fills her home with a wide array of items, including a Hello Kitty curling iron, telephone, waffle maker, countertop water dispenser, giant television remote, and even a microscope, her plastic Hello Kitty figurines and plush dominate many bookshelves in two different countries. "I have about 150 plushes here in the U.S. and another 100 back in Asia," she says. Marie Angeline lists as her favorites the tokidoki plush, her Hello Kitty M•A•C plush, her Macy's 150th anniversary Hello Kitty plush, and a giant Hello Kitty plush wearing bronze shoes and holding a bouquet. Her smallest? "I have the 2½ inch McDonald's Gem Colored Hello Kitty collection on display."

Whatever size and shape these fans' collections may take, they all share a passion for keeping Hello Kitty present in their lives.

GO, HELLO KITTY, GO!

Hello Kitty travels! From auto accessories—such as air fresheners, floor mats, antennae toppers, and license plate frames—to tricycles, folding bicycles, golf clubs, and surfboards, she has something for everyone.

Hello Kitty cars, double-decker buses, taxi cabs, and scooters have appeared all around the world. In 1999, Japan's Daihatsu Motor Co. debuted the Mira Hello Kitty car, complete with Hello Kitty grille ornament, hubcaps, key, and dashboard details. Hello Kitty also made her debut on a Yamaha Vino limited edition scooter, for which a Hello Kitty helmet was also available.

Down under, Australian fan Vicky P. threw herself a Hello Kitty–themed birthday party (complete with a "pin the bow on Hello Kitty" game) and treated herself to Hello Kitty vanity license plates.

Taking things even further, Malaysian Hello Kitty fan Mohd A. decorated his van tires-to-sunroof in Hello Kitty. Not only did he stock it with store-bought accessories, he also reupholstered the car seats and stylized the steering wheel in pink Hello Kitty printed fabric.

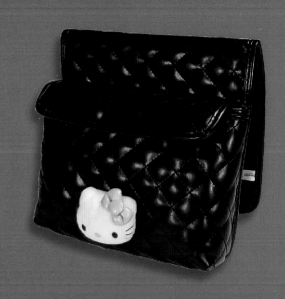

TOP DRAWER HELLO KITTY

Sitting atop and filling desks worldwide are Hello Kitty school and office supplies, quite possibly her most celebrated and sought-after collectibles category, with a veritable rainbow of stickers and decorative pens and pencils available. Worker bees, pen pals, teachers, artists, and students can all agree that Hello Kitty makes getting the job done more fun!

Many collections may begin with a single pencil or fruit-scented eraser (which smell so delicious, some admirers have reportedly tasted them). From the one piece, a desktop or dresser drawer slowly fills with Hello Kitty paper clips, push-pins, sticky note pads, agendas, calculators, staplers, folders, memo cubes, clipboards, tape, stationery, and on and on. Each January, resolute fans can start with a clean slate with the latest Hello Kitty wall calendar.

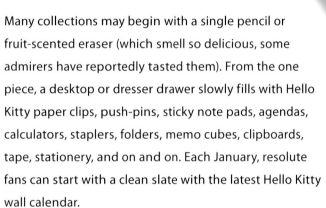

HELLO KITTY SLEEPS OVER

HELLO KITTY'S PAPER KISS

NOTEBOOK

HELLOKITTY

ぬりえ

シールつき！

What's new?

HELLO KITTY

Bookworms go crazy for Hello Kitty book offerings. Favorites have included a Japanese limited edition *My Kitty* book, published by Asukashinsha to celebrate Hello Kitty's 25th anniversary. The book included a year-by-year guide to her collectibles, how-tos for drawing Hello Kitty, and perforated sheets for use as calling cards or luggage tags. Other favorites include *Hello Kitty Everywhere*, a photo and haiku book of her adventures; *Hello Kitty's Little Book of Big Ideas*, a book about studying and sleepovers; and *Hello Kitty, Hello USA! A Celebration of All Fifty States*.

Hello Kitty Hello Everything!
25 Years of Fun!

Hello Kitty
Hello USA!
A Celebration of All Fifty States

Hello Kitty
little book of big ideas
a girl's guide to brains, beauty, fashion, friendship & fun!
by marie y. moss

Hello Kitty Everywhere!
PHOTOGRAPHS AND HAIKU

HELLO, HIGH-TECH

Over the years, Sanrio has kept Hello Kitty on the cutting edge with gadgets that keep fans connected. In 1996, one of her very first forays into the high-tech realm came via photo-sticker booths. Sanrio acquired many of these arcade-style machines to feature inside their stores.

Then came the simultaneous launches of Hello Kitty cell phones that included a handset Hello Kitty face phone with a matching case, a Versa "Shake Music Free" phone that offered song-skipping capabilities simply by shaking the phone, a Hello Kitty Nokia 6010 pay-as-you-go phone, and even Hello Kitty Bluetooth headsets. Next came texting, as Sanrio launched the official Hello Kitty Text Messenger.

Dubbed the "cuter computer," Sanrio teamed with Epson to launch a Hello Kitty Epson wide note laptop computer that fans could accessorize with a Hello Kitty mouse, mousepad, or even a mimobot USB flash drive. Hello Kitty fans were also technologically tempted by the Millennium Hello Kitty Multi-Media Personal Computer. And for gamers, there came the Hello Kitty Dreamcast console by Sega, sold with games *Hello Kitty's Dream Passport* and *Hello Kitty's Garden*. In the years since, many new video games have been released. Titles have included Game Boy's *Hello Kitty: Happy Party Pals*; PlayStation's *Hello Kitty Simple 1500 series*; and Nintendo DS's *Hello Kitty: Big City Dreams*.

Next up were assorted digital camera offerings. Styles have included a Hello Kitty megapixel digital camera with three changeable faceplates, and a Hello Kitty digital camera shaped like her face, with the camera lens hidden inside her hair bow. There's even a Hello Kitty Flip Mino camcorder from Pure Digital Technologies. Weighing just over three ounces, the super-portable and USB-accessible device lets fans record and share their stories in video form. In 2009, Sanrio announced several Hello Kitty applications for iPhone and iPod touch, making it easy for fans to join in her 35th anniversary celebration and keep up to date.

Hello Kitty has appeared in film and television as well. In 1986, *Hello Kitty's Furry Tale Theatre* debuted on the Family Channel in English and on Univision translated into Spanish. Additional Japanese and American animated Hello Kitty programs included *Hello Kitty's Paradise* and *Hello Kitty and Friends*. In 2005, Sanrio debuted Hello Kitty's claymation series *Stump Village* featuring Hello Kitty alongside other Sanrio characters. In 2006, a similarly themed, computer-animated series debuted: *The Adventures of Hello Kitty and Friends*. The collection of fifty-two CGI episodes features Hello Kitty alongside Sanrio characters not traditionally seen with her, including Keroppi, the Donut Pond resident who plays baseball; and Badtz-Maru, the mischievous penguin from Gorgeoustown.

But as high-tech as it gets is the Hello Kitty ROBO, a robot companion programmed with 20,000 conversation patterns and voice recognition capabilities for up to ten people. This futuristic girl reacts when lifted and has movable head, arms, and whiskers that shine whenever she expresses emotion. A microphone concealed in her bow allows her to speak, sing, and tell time; and after recognizing her owner through a camera in her eyes, she can then call her owner by name. At about $3,700, ROBO may well be the *ultimate* Hello Kitty collectible!

Visit Hello Kitty on the Internet at www.sanrio.com, an online home for all Sanrio characters, and check your favorite social networking sites for Hello Kitty's official profile.

MUSICAL INSPIRATION

Hello Kitty has many fans from the music industry, in genres ranging from pop to rock to hip-hop to country. She can also be found on musical instruments of her own. Among those notable music fans is Japanese pop idol Tomomi Kahara, a quirky diva who is often seen wearing Hello Kitty jewelry and hair accessories while on tour, modeling true "Kitty-lah" style.

Another fan is singer and songwriter Lisa Loeb, who in 2002 released the album *Hello Lisa*, complete with cover art depicting Hello Kitty wearing Loeb's signature cat-eyed glasses. The album was celebrated with a tour that included several autographing sessions at Sanrio stores across the country, as well as an appearance by Loeb and Hello Kitty at the Japanese MTV Music Awards. Loeb's pal Dweezil Zappa even helped produce a music video for her song "Underdog," which features a gingham-clad Hello Kitty. She appears playing an acoustic guitar on Loeb's kitchen counter while the singer waits for toast to pop out of her Hello Kitty toaster (the rest of her kitchen is covered in Hello Kitty appliances and finds).

Iconic Grammy-winning singer-songwriter Mariah Carey is equally smitten with Hello Kitty collectibles. In fact, she owns two of the most coveted Hello Kitty collectibles out there: a Hello Kitty Stratocaster guitar and a Hello Kitty Dreadnought acoustic guitar, both by Fender. Accessories available for the instruments include Hello Kitty guitar picks, gig bags, and guitar straps.

Japanese pop singer and actress Ayumi Hamasaki was offered the ultimate opportunity for any Hello Kitty fan when Sanrio invited her to collaborate on a limited edition line. The result was a mix of highly collectible items—key chains, stationery, crafty homemade-like dolls, cell phone straps, and more—featuring an Ayumi-esque, cartoon girl rockin' out.

Visitors to Tokyo's Ginza district can sing their hearts out inside Big Echo's Hello Kitty karaoke room. And fans anywhere can make their own "big echo" by lip-synching to Hello Kitty's debut album *Hello World*, released in Fall 2008. The CD is comprised of eleven tracks performed by various artists including Keke Palmer.

HELLO KITTY SHINES

From twinkling tiaras to rings and things, Hello Kitty gems and jewelry have proven from the start to be some of the most sought after pieces. Designer collaborations with Kimora Lee Simmons, Tarina Tarantino, Judith Leiber, and Swarovski™ Crystal helped set the stage for positioning Hello Kitty accessories as serious-with-a-smile, real-deal bling.

Tarina Tarantino had been a Hello Kitty fan and admirer of Japanese style for over thirty years. In 2002, she collaborated on a jewelry collection with Sanrio. The union resulted in Pink Head, a Hello Kitty incarnation inspired by Tarantino's own bright pink hair. The designs soon gained popularity among many of Hello Kitty's celebrity fans.

Equally eye-catching are Judith Leiber's Swarovski crystal-encrusted items, including the Hello Kitty Minaudiere mini clutch, which first retailed for $1,900, and the $30,000 platinum-and-diamond tiara she designed especially for Hello Kitty's 30th anniversary year.

Fashion mogul Kimora Lee Simmons debuted her Kimora Lee Simmons for Hello Kitty Collection in March 2005 and has since gone on to design some of Hello Kitty's most coveted collectibles, including necklace pendants, watches, and rings. With collectible themes including Glam Kitty, Simply Kitty, Princess Kitty, and Zodiac Kitty, the designer's creations appeal to the tens of thousands of glamour girls worldwide who line up for trunk shows at Sanrio shops and jewelry stores where limited edition pieces are often sold.

As Simmons herself puts it, "Hello Kitty has charmed us for decades by reminding us of life's little pleasures; friendship, kindness, wonder, and playfulness. Kimora Lee Simmons for Hello Kitty was created for women who want to cherish the lighter side of life. This limited edition collection celebrates our enduring love for Hello Kitty and the smiles she brings, with spectacular diamonds because life should sparkle."

Among the most devoted is Debi C. of Michigan, a collector who wears Hello Kitty jewelry every day. Like many fans of Simmons's designs, Debi adores the Zodiac Kitty line the best, collecting not only her own birth sign, but many others as well. "My Glam Kitty necklace—a recent Valentine's Day gift . . . well, I still can't believe it is mine!" Debi says. She has also acquired pieces of Tarantino's designs; she treasures her Russian Kitty pendant necklaces and her Lolita Kitty locket.

Hello Kitty's sparkliest creation is the Super Hello Kitty Jewel Doll, created in celebration of her 35th anniversary by Sanrio, Swarovski, and Japanese jewelry designer I.K. This Hello Kitty doll, covered in jewels, made her first public appearance at the renowned Baselworld jewelry show in Switzerland and is studded with a 1.027-carat diamond on her ribbon, 403 pink sapphires on her body, citrine on her nose, black spinels on her eyes, and a total of 1,939 white topaz on her head. The price tag: $150,000,000!

Helping to celebrate Hello Kitty's 35th anniversary, Tokyo-based design collective Ambush collaborated with Sanrio on their signature superhero "POW" necklaces, featuring Hello Kitty.

HELLO KITTY, HELLO STYLE

Hello Kitty may have made her debut in a seated pose, but she has certainly gotten the world to stand up and take notice of her fun-spirited style. Her clothing lines are no exception. Sanrio has translated her playful personality into supercute fashion offerings worn worldwide.

Trendsetters look to Hello Kitty for inspiration. Her style offers innocence with a wink. It is a nod to what's hot with a bit of humor and happiness, possessing a *je ne sais quoi* quality that makes it impossible to place in a single category. Safe yet cutting edge. Prepster yet punk. Whatever the desired statement, Hello Kitty's collections function as fashion mood rings for her fans, a way to show their true colors. She is the all-accepting friend who encourages individual style. Drawn in by her wide-eyed "take a chance" energy, fans are trying on the trends with complete confidence, because anything is possible with Hello Kitty by your side.

In fact, when her accessories first burst onto the style scene back in the 1970s, they were immediately embraced by girls of all ages. And as those accessories evolved into ready-to-wear clothing lines, the world was ready to wear whatever Hello Kitty offered. From her earlier mittens, shoes, and tote bags to today's twenty-first-century take on trends, Hello Kitty's style sensibility has been universal from the get-go.

THE STRAWBERRY STORY

Long before Sanrio had Hello Kitty, it had strawberries. The company's first product prominently featured red and pink strawberries. Shoppers found it refreshing to see such cheerful patterns in stores at a time when such designs were rare. Today, strawberries continue to play a role in the Hello Kitty story—she has her magazine, *Strawberry News*; a series of strawberry-themed products that debuted in 1997; and the motif for one of her fashion lines.

When written in *Kanji* (Japanese writing using Chinese-derived characters), "strawberry" includes the character for "mother." Accordingly, the berry is widely considered sweet, warm, and nurturing—making it a perfect symbol for Sanrio, whose philosophy is built on similar characteristics.

THE FABULOUS LIFE OF THE GIRL

Take a peek at some of Hello Kitty's most memorable fashion and beauty moments:

🍎 Designers Richie Rich and Traver Rains of Heatherette have long been Hello Kitty fans. Rich and Rains featured Hello Kitty in their first New York Fashion Week show in 2002, and launched the Hello Kitty by Heatherette collection of fashion and accessories in 2003.

🍎 Fashion show producers Oliver Dow and Darren Greenblatt took 7th on Sixth by storm with their long-running "Girls Rule!" fashion show for the teen market. In 2003, Hello Kitty accessories decorated many of the designs, with Hello Kitty treats on the seats for buyers and editors.

Hello Kitty is more at home in fans' homes than ever, thanks to the launch of Momoberry by Sanrio, a collection of upscale items including home décor and fragrances.

Body Velvet
6 fl. oz./180 ml
©1976, 2006 SANRIO

Body Velvet
2 fl. oz./60 ml
©1976, 2006 SANRIO

Momoberry by Sanrio

th Bubbles
2 fl. oz./355 ml
©1976, 2006 SANRIO

Bath Bubbles
2 fl. oz./60 ml
©1976, 2006 SANRIO

Shower Dream
8 fl. oz./236 ml
©1976, 2006 SANRIO

Shower Dream
2 fl. oz./60 ml
©1976, 2006 SANRIO

- Actress Tori Spelling and her pet pug Mimi La Rue turned out to celebrate the 2005 launch of Hello Kitty by Little Lily, a collection of fashion for dogs designed by Lara Alameddine and Daniel Dubiecki.

- Anna Sui collaborated with Sanrio on a collection of Hello Kitty plush, accessories, and stationery in 2007.

- In 2008, Japanese *Vogue* devoted editorial coverage to a fashion spread wherein Hello Kitty models the John Galliano for Dior spring collection.

- Bicoastal boutique design house Opening Ceremony featured Japanese culture in its Fall 2008 line, celebrating the occasion by installing Hello Kitty's house in the middle of its Los Angeles and New York City boutiques, with Hello Kitty collectibles for sale inside.

In Fall '08, Sanrio opened the Sanrio Luxe boutique located in New York City's Times Square. The concept shop offers collectibles with a more sophisticated touch. Fancy is the décor, with black crystal chandeliers and black and white modern romantic fixtures. And fancy is the merchandise, with upscale items from collaborations with designers such as Victoria Couture (from Paris), Camomilla (for high-end Italian leather shoes and accessories), and Kimora Lee Simmons's sparkly diamond jewelry designs. Sanrio Luxe also offers collectors the opportunity to purchase items from around the world.

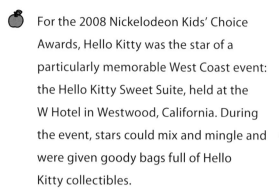

For the 2008 Nickelodeon Kids' Choice Awards, Hello Kitty was the star of a particularly memorable West Coast event: the Hello Kitty Sweet Suite, held at the W Hotel in Westwood, California. During the event, stars could mix and mingle and were given goody bags full of Hello Kitty collectibles.

In 2009, M•A•C Cosmetics debuted the M•A•C Cosmetics Hello Kitty Colour Collection and the more upscale Hello Kitty Kouture Collection. The collections featured various pink shades, with a generous sprinkling of sparkle throughout. Limited edition packaging was offered, featuring facial powder compacts with Swarovski™ crystal details. Accompanying the pretty palettes were limited edition accessories including makeup bags, brush holders, a charm bracelet, and a Hello Kitty plush.

Helping to celebrate the launch, thirty designers were enlisted to create one-of-a-kind Hello Kitty fashions that were auctioned off to benefit the Museum at the Fashion Institute of Technology in New York City. Designers included Charlotte Ronson, Herve Leger by Max Azria, Catherine Malandrino, and Zac Posen. A couture Hello Kitty corset was designed for the cause by Phillipe and David Blond of The Blonds label. Songstress Katy Perry wore the corset for a walk down the red carpet at the 2009 Brit Awards and later up to the stage to accept the award for Best International Female.

Hello Kitty tees are perennially popular, but two all-time favorites are the "I ♥ Nerds" collection by Mighty Fine and the "Adopt A Friend" limited edition T-shirt depicting Hello Kitty with a puppy tucked under her arm. Proceeds from the sale of this shirt benefitted the Humane Society of the United States.

IT'S IN THE BAG

Wherever Hello Kitty fans' days may take them, there's a bag perfect for the journey. Hello Kitty can be found on wallets and purses, totes and makeup bags, laptop cases, rolling luggage, and more—suited for everything from an afternoon of shopping to a Saturday sleepover to a two-week trip abroad. And what fits inside those carryalls is equally smile inducing: From packs of gum and tissue to protective cases for gadgets and gear, the perfectly packed bag holds plenty of room for Hello Kitty.

contact lens case

scented pen

compact and comb set

cell phone charm

business card holder

bandages and tissues

stamp ring

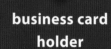

coin purse

sunglasses case

memo pad

nail file

key ring
(plus house, bike lock,
and roller skate keys)

gum

iPhone case
(plus phone!)

A suitcase here for stationery sets and pen pal letters . . . a tote there for origami papers, ribbons, and wrappings . . . Hello Kitty handbags, purses, luggage, and travel tags come in all shapes and sizes. Beading, faux fur, metallic fabrics, and quilting have all been used as a backdrop for Hello Kitty's image. For daytime, a Hello Kitty tote or messenger-style bag can stow an afternoon's worth of necessities. For weekends away, fans can grab a Hello Kitty backpack or structured suitcase. Drop a snack into a Hello Kitty Zip Seal Sandwich Bag and you're ready to go.

Beyond luggage, girls have been collecting Hello Kitty luggage tags since before she even appeared in the United States. Standout tags include die-cut airplanes and apples, and colorful tags with metallic rainbows and Hawaiian settings.

UBIQUITOUS GIRL

Thanks to her uncanny knack for spreading smiles wherever she goes, Sanrio continues to send Hello Kitty on ever-bigger ventures, sharing the love with people around the world. Sometimes these ventures are larger than life.

THE WORLD'S LARGEST STORE

ONE WAY

HERALD SQ West 35th St

At 33.6-feet tall, 34.8-feet wide and 45-feet long, Hello Kitty's Macy's Thanksgiving Day Parade balloon was one of the largest Hello Kitty figures ever created. It takes eighty handlers to steer the Supercute Hello Kitty balloon down and around the streets of New York City.

Guests of the Hello Kitty suite at one of Japan's Daiwa Royal Hotel locations can enjoy seeing her in more terrestrial form, including posing on all of the sink-side toiletries.

In 2006, the Hau Sheng Hospital in Taipei, Taiwan, turned to Hello Kitty to welcome and swaddle newborns. In a makeover of their thirty-bed maternity ward, everything from nurses' uniforms and baby blankets to bedside phones and even elevator doors were bedecked with Hello Kitty's image.

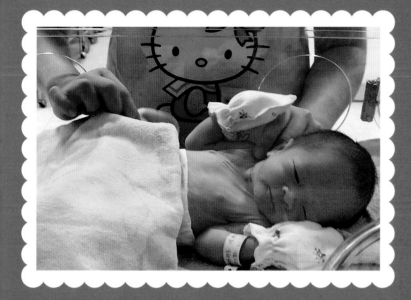

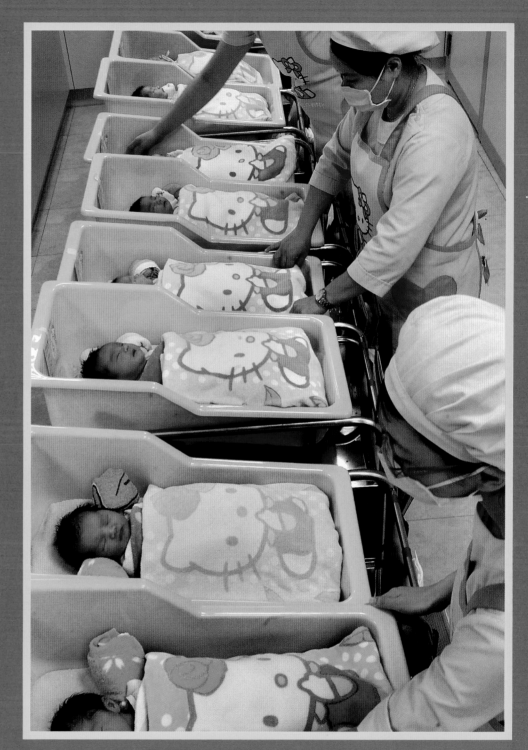

Taiwan is also home to the Hello Kitty Sweets theme cafés, where everything from the décor to the dishes honor the global icon. Fans flip for the Hello Kitty banquette booths and placemats, Hello Kitty hamburgers (featuring buns in the shape of her head), and the sweet Hello Kitty–shaped desserts for dine-in or takeout. Even the Hello Kitty napkins and paper coasters are popular souvenirs.

Taiwanese airline Eva Air got into the act as well, fashioning two Hello Kitty Airbus jets, complete with Hello Kitty and her friends painted on the exteriors, Hello Kitty–themed food served in flight, and Hello Kitty flight attendant uniforms, boarding passes, and waiting area. The airline was declared "Best Livery" in 2007 by *Wallpaper* magazine for its innovation and whimsical take on air travel design.

Hello Kitty boardfest Huntington Beach

Hello Kitty appears on giant goggles and skis at Heavens Sonohara Ski Resort in Nagano, Japan, home of the 1998 XVIII Olympic Winter Games. Hello Kitty was a part of Boardfest, an all-girl surfing competition and beach party event in Huntington Beach, California, co-sponsored by Sanrio. Hello Kitty sand tents, surfboards, and D.J. booth brought *kawaii* (Japanese for "cute") to the event. And indoor athletes can hit the Ikebukuro Brunswick Sports Garden bowling alley in Japan, where visitors are treated to Hello Kitty alley art and bowling balls.

In 1983, Hello Kitty was named child ambassador for the United Nations Children's Fund (aka UNICEF, the global organization that provides long-term aid to children and mothers in developing countries). And in 2004, she was given the exclusive title of UNICEF Special Friend of Children, as Sanrio donated proceeds to the organization and distributed information for fans eager to contribute and learn more about its humanitarian efforts.

Closer to home, Hello Kitty promotes friendship in the shopping mall any time a child helps another create her own plush pal. In 2006, Build-A-Bear Workshop added Hello Kitty to its make-your-own plush program. Customers can dress their 17-inch Hello Kitty plush, in Hello Kitty clothes, pajamas, shoes and accessories. The collection even includes a Hello Kitty plush-sized upholstered chair. Then, in 2007, Mattel's Hello Kitty Barbie appeared. Her striped top and dark denim jeans were paired with a white Hello Kitty jacket and a pink Hello Kitty belt, charm necklace, and purse.

The Madame Alexander Doll Company created its own dolls inspired by Hello Kitty. In 2006, Madame Alexander offered the Ice Cream Delight Hello Kitty doll set packaged with a plush Hello Kitty shaped like an ice cream cone with a cherry on top of her head, as well as "My New Friend Hello Kitty" sets with kimono-clad dolls. In 2007, Wendy Loves Hello Kitty City hit store shelves along with the plaid-clad "Punk Princess Hello Kitty Wendy" doll sets. In 2009, Madame Alexander went "Out and About with Hello Kitty," a set wherein the doll and Hello Kitty wore matching pink coats.

That same year, Hello Kitty Studio opened its castle-like doors to their fairytale portrait studio in Shanghai, China. Fans take a seat with a larger-than-life Hello Kitty—who wears a variety of outfits—on overstuffed and tufted couches and chairs in front of colorful, dreamy backdrops.

Colorful and dreamy backdrops were just one element of "Kitty Ex," or the 2004 Hello Kitty Exhibition, a collaborative art exhibit executed by Japan's Iwami Art Museum in conjunction with Sanrio. It consisted of works by a collection of international artists who found their inspiration in the celebration of Hello Kitty's 30th anniversary. Favorite contributions included *Hotel Kittyfornia*, a film by French fashion designer Jean-Charles de Castelbajac, that features a model filmed all over Paris donning a giant Hello Kitty head; fashion label/art collective/creative team Surface to Air's 50-yard crop-circle work of art designed on a carefully selected stretch of land near Stonehenge, directly below the flight path to Heathrow Airport; fashion designer Jeremy Scott's "Hello De Milo" statue showing Hello Kitty as the Venus de Milo; and Japanese artist Nagi Noda's plush creation that was half Hello Kitty and half panda bear. Other artists who contributed to the exhibition included graffiti artist Ryan McGinley, musicians Sean Lennon and Malcolm McLaren, and Japanese graphic artist Kazunari Hattori. A small collection of limited edition gift shop items were designed by some of the artists exclusively for the exhibit.

American sculptor Tom Sachs has created many of his works in homage to Hello Kitty. From Barneys New York's Madison Avenue holiday windows that involved a Chanel-clad Hello Kitty as an integral part of a nativity scene in 1994, to a twenty-one-foot bronze Hello Kitty wind-up doll and a seven-foot Hello Kitty bronze fountain that held court first at New York City's Lever House on Park Avenue in 2008 (then traveled to Aspen and Paris), Sachs has found much inspiration in Hello Kitty.

For those who prefer reading about Hello Kitty, the European *Hello Kitty Magazine* is a photo-driven monthly. Each issue is packaged with a small gift. The publication celebrates a different international location each month, including bits of history, travel information, and photos of collectibles. The premiere issue, a celebration of all things English, hit newsstands in July 2007 and sold out quickly—perhaps in part due to the accompanying charm bracelet and travel pouch. Sanrio's *Strawberry News* monthly magazine celebrates Hello Kitty in addition to other popular Sanrio characters, and likewise includes a small gift with purchase. Hello Kitty also finds monthly mentions in *Convex*, a Japanese style magazine that often includes gifts as well.

Selling out faster than most other Happy Meal promotions (in Taiwan, lines form down the block), Hello Kitty items at McDonald's have included digital watches shaped like apples, plush Hello Kitty dangling key chains, hula-hooping mechanical Hello Kitty figurines, and super cute, twist-top Hello Kitty containers, with miniature school supplies.

HELLO, THEME PARKS

The ultimate destination for any Hello Kitty fan is a trip to Japan to visit Sanrio's indoor theme park Puroland, and Harmonyland, its outdoor counterpart. Puroland opened in Tama City, Tokyo, in December 1990. Its most popular attraction is the character boat ride, though shopping for limited edition products and other souvenirs in Puroland's Festival Plaza runs a close second on most visitors' must-do list. And when it's snack time, Puroland's traditional Japanese pastry, Ningyoyaki, is a fan favorite.

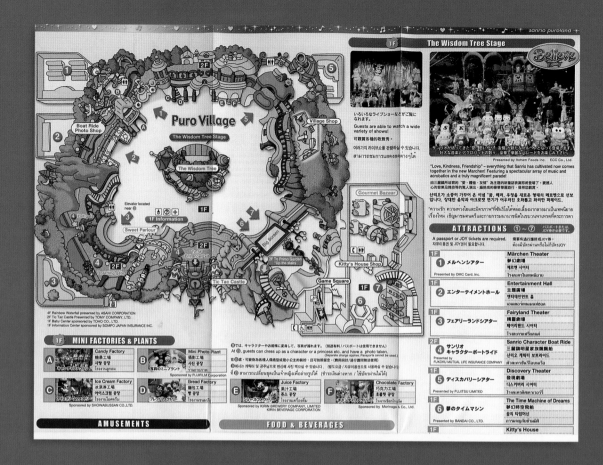

① Sofa
Sit on the sofa.... Relax and enjoy Kitty's pretty piano playing.

② Painting
Admire the painting from different angles and...!

③ TV Phone
When Kitty's family calls, make sure you pick it up!

④ Kitchen Door
What's on the other side of the door? Peek through the keyhole and see Kitty and Mimmy baking cookies.

⑤ TV
Featuring the hit TV shows "KITTO HIT RANKING" and "QUIZ ATTACK DON." Don't miss them!

⑥ Make-up Mirror
Peer into the mirror, and look deep into your own eyes....

⑦ Personal Computer
Use the touch screen and play fun-filled Sanrio character computer g

⑧ Closet
An adorable teddy bear is sitting on the closet. Go up to him!

⑨ Shower
What happens when you go up to the Kitty-shaped bathtub?

⑩ Papa and Mama's Room
Approach Papa and Mama's room. Can you hear Papa and Mama having a cheerful chat?

⑪ Bookshelf
If you happen to find a book sticking out, do Kitty a favor and push it

Harmonyland, which opened in April 1991, celebrates many of Sanrio's characters, though Hello Kitty's presence is quite prominent. Located in Oita Prefecture in Kyushu, Japan, the open-air theme park offers rides, an arcade, and live character shows. Favorite attractions include a tea-cup ride and carousel wherein the "cups" and "cages" are designed to look like Sanrio characters, a visit inside Hello Kitty's house where Hello Kitty is waiting to greet fans, and an evening show that finds Hello Kitty performing as a water fairy among brightly colored, booming fireworks.

Grace L. of California had always dreamed of a trip to Puroland, and with enough pennies saved, she finally made the journey. Her favorite attraction was a replica of Hello Kitty's Victorian-style house, where she explored all of the rooms. After the house tour, Grace and other guests waited in line to have their picture taken with Hello Kitty. Later, being true to the Victorian era, Grace sat for an artist who created a silhouette cutout of her profile facing Hello Kitty's. The picture was then placed in a souvenir Puroland frame. While Grace swears she would make a return visit just for the Hello Kitty–shaped crackers, perhaps the reason for her next Puroland trip would be to purchase the Anna Sui Hello Kitty platform sandals she reluctantly left behind in one of the Hello Kitty shops.

Heading to Puroland from Dusseldorf in December 2004, Achim F. and Andrea S. were planning to return with souvenir-packed suitcases—and an official Puroland marriage certificate! Andrea had been a Hello Kitty fan for years when she met Achim, and they visited Puroland together in 2000. It was then that they discovered the possibility of getting married—reception and all—at Puroland.

As a blogger devoted to finding and sharing the next big Hello Kitty find, Andrea has always been motivated by the notion that just around the corner, or across international divides, lies the opportunity to discover the next great Hello Kitty collectible. Even Achim is in on the act, sharing his philosophy on a Hello Kitty fan's never-ending search for what's new. "What we like about Hello Kitty is that even in the strangest place on earth, you are able to find something you haven't seen before," he says. "For example, if you are a fan of Prada and you have all the money in the world, you can go to a store and buy the whole collection. With Hello Kitty this is different. Even in a small toy store in the Netherlands you can find something that someone living in Tokyo has not seen before. This makes it interesting."

Upon discovering that a Puroland marriage is not officially recognized, Andrea and Achim scrambled to tie the knot two days prior, with the help of the German embassy based in Japan. This allowed them to freely enjoy every detail of their Puroland nuptials, including a day dressed in Hello Kitty wedding couture designed by Andrea herself. As an added bonus, the couple discovered that they were the first Western couple to say "I do" in Puroland.

Brides can also opt to be married at the Japanese Daiichi Hotel. The Princess Hello Kitty package includes a ready-to-wed Hello Kitty wedding dress.

Grace G. of Pennsylvania began collecting Sanrio items as a child living in the Philippines. When she got engaged in 2003, and with a Pennsylvania-to-Puroland trip not in the cards, she found herself drawn to Dear Daniel collectibles and the character's courtship with Hello Kitty. So taken by the pair, she added Hello Kitty and Dear Daniel collectibles to many of her wedding festivities. Grace's bridal shower featured a Hello Kitty banner, cake topper, and Hello Kitty cosmetics favors for attendees. Shower gifts included Hello Kitty kitchenware like sake cups, teapots, and cookie cutters. One of Grace's favorite wedding souvenirs is a Hello Kitty bride and Dear Daniel groom figure spinning to Wagner's "Wedding March" atop a collectible music box. Next on her special occasion agenda? "A grown-up Hello Kitty–themed birthday party for myself!" says Grace.

HELLO, FUTURE!

In the future, one thing's for certain: Hello Kitty is sure to continue spreading happiness, friendship, fun, and *kawaii* all around the world.

HELLO, MARIE!

Marie Moss is the author of *Hello Kitty's Little Book of Big Ideas* and *Hello Kitty, Hello Everything*. She is the former fashion director for *Seventeen Magazine* and has appeared as a style expert on many national television programs including *The Oprah Winfrey Show*, CNN and *The View*. She is co-founder of M & B Vintage.

Moss has been smitten with Hello Kitty for as long as she can remember. Her favorite collectibles are her Hello Kitty digital watch with interchangeable outfits and her Hello Kitty travel trinket box. Her daughter, Maisy, is equally charmed by Hello Kitty, and they share their Hello Kitty–filled house with Moss's husband, Stephen, and their mixed-breed dog, Harriet Dixie.

ACKNOWLEDGMENTS

A big thank you to Linh Nguyen Forse at Sanrio, Kristin Mehus-Roe and Amy Wideman for the dream-come-true opportunity to write this book in celebration of all things Hello Kitty, and to Jessica Eskelsen and Kasey Free for their expertise. Thanks, too, to Bill Hensley for the shout-out that started it all, and to the fabulous fans around the world who shared their stories and collections.

A big hug to Mom for always nurturing—and celebrating—my need to collect, to Stephen for finding humor in Hello Kitty kitchenware, to Barri for being my sidekick in style, to Marianne for "count on me" mall trips to see Hello Kitty's latest offerings (who knew those excursions were actually field research?!), and to my girl, my love, Maisy, who has taught me how to truly appreciate the little things in life.

IMAGE CREDITS AND SPECIAL THANKS

Every effort has been made to trace copyright holders. If any unintended omissions have been made, becker&mayer! would be pleased to add appropriate acknowledgment in future editions.

All images are courtesy and copyright © 1976, 2010 Sanrio Co., Ltd. unless otherwise noted below:

Page 25: Photo courtesy of Maria Fleischman

Page 27: All photos courtesy of Emily Hirai

Page 48: (top right) Yoshikazu Tsuno/AFP/Getty Images

Page 49: (right) Photo courtesy of Hideya Hamano

Page 56: (left) Yoshikazu Tsuno/AFP/Getty Images; (right) Toru Yamanaka/AFP/Getty Images

Page 57: (left) Yoshikazu Tsuno/AFP/Getty Images

Page 60: (left) Yoshikazu Tsuno/AFP/Getty Images

Page 61: (right) Yoshikazu Tsuno/AFP/Getty Images

Page 62: Koichi Kamoshida/Getty Images

Page 63: (center) AP Photo/Akira Ono

Page 76: (left) Vince Bucci/Getty Images

Page 78: (left) Eric Neitzel/WireImage for Little Lily, Inc.

Page 82: All photos by Todd Williamson/WireImage

Page 84: (right) Mike Marsland/WireImage

Page 95: (top and bottom left) Sam Yeh/AFP/Getty Images

Page 100: (right) Eric Neitzel/WireImage for Orsi Public Relations

Page 102: (center) Yoshikazu Tsuno/AFP/Getty Images

Page 105: All photos by Toru Yamanaka/AFP/Getty Images

Page 106: (left) Andrew H. Walker/Getty Images; (center) Sipa via AP Images; (right) Photo courtesy of Marie Moss

Page 107: magazines courtesy of Marie Moss

Page 109: (top left) AP Photo/Vincent Yu

Page 118: (bottom left) Photo courtesy of Grace Lin

Page 119: (left) photo courtesy of Andrea Stolzenberger and Achim Fettig

Page 120: All photos courtesy of Grace Guevarra-Giagnocavo

Christian Lau: pages 24 (left), 28 (left), 44 (top), 69 (right), 87 (center)

Sarah Golonka: misc. photos throughout

Adam Wallacavage: misc. photos throughout

Sanrio would like to extend special thanks to the following for their assistance in providing images:

Sanrio Co., Ltd. Japan

Sanrio Wave Hong Kong

Sanrio Taiwan

Sanrio Shanghai

Puroland

Harmonyland

Nakajima USA, Inc.

Special Thanks

Janet Hsu	Dave Marchi
Daniel Inoue	Dan Peters
Ken Yamamoto	Susan Tran
Jill Koch	Michelle Miyashiro
Jennifer Campbell	Tomoko Tokuya

Legal Notices

Trademarks, logo marks, and brand names used and displayed are the registered trademarks or unregistered trademarks of Sanrio Co., Ltd. or of third parties. If any unintended omissions have been made, becker&mayer! would be pleased to add appropriate notice in future editions.

Daihatsu® is a registered trademark of Daihatsu Motor Co., Ltd. Fender® and Stratocaster® are registered trademarks of Fender Musical Instruments Corporation. Barbie® is a registered trademark of Mattel, Inc. My Little Pony® is a registered trademark of Hasbro, Inc. McDonald's® and Happy Meal™ are registered trademarks of McDonald's Corporation. Paul Frank and Julius the Monkey © Paul Frank Industries®. tokidoki © 2009 tokidoki LLC. MasterCard® is a registered trademark of MasterCard Worldwide. M·A·C® is a registered trademark of M·A·C, Make-up Artists Cosmetics Inc. iPhone® and iPod® are registered trademarks of Apple Computer, Inc. PEZ® is a registered trademark of PEZ Candy, Inc. Sega® and Dreamcast® are registered trademarks of the SEGA Corporation. atmos™ is © 2010 atmos-tokyo. Macy's® is a registered trademark of Macy's, Inc. (Formerly known as Federated Department Stores, Inc.). Vino® is a registered trademark of Yamaha Corporatation. Versa® is a registered trademark of Nissan Motor Co. Ltd. Nokia® is a registered trademark of Nokia Corporation. Bluetooth® is a registered trademark of Bluetooth SIG, Inc. EPSON® is a registered trademark of Seiko Epson Corporation. MIMOBOT® is a registered trademark of Mimoco, Inc. Millennium® is a registered trademark of Samsung Corp. PlayStation® is a registered trademark of Sony Computer Entertainment, Inc. Nintendo DS® and Gameboy® are registered trademarks of Nintendo. Swarovski® is a registered trademark of Swarovski AG. Judith Leiber® is a registered trademark of Judith Leiber, LLC. Kimora Lee Simmons™ is © Kimora Lee Simmons, 2010. Tarina Tarantino™ is © Tarina Tarantino, 2010. Betsey Johnson™ is © 2010 Betsey Johnson. Comcast® is a registered trademark of Comcast Corporation. EVA Air® is a registered trademark of Eva Airways. Brunswick® is a registered trademark of Brunswick Corp. Build-A-Bear Workshop® is a registered trademark of Build-A-Bear Retail Management, Inc. Madame Alexander® is a registered trademark of the Alexander Doll Co., Inc. All rights reserved. Any usage of these terms anywhere in this book is done so simply for editorial purposes and does not indicate any endorsement by or affiliation with these entities, none of which participated in the production of this book.